White Doe

Other books by John Repp:

Thirst Like This (1990, University of Missouri Press)
The Fertile Crescent (2004, Cherry Grove Collections)

White Doe

POEMS

John Repp

Mayapple Press 2004

Published by   MAYAPPLE PRESS
                  408 N. Lincoln St.
                  Bay City, MI 48708
                  www.mayapplepress.com

ISBN 0-932412-27-0

Thanks to the editors of publications in which earlier versions of the following poems first appeared:

Comstock Review: "Then We Seemed Woven Talk"
Confluence: "Maxine Dancing"
The Journal: "I Want to Buy This House"
Eleven Bulls: "The Mouse and the Broom"

A sabbatical leave from the English & Theatre Arts Department at Edinboro University of Pennsylvania provided time crucial to the writing of this collection.

This book was typeset by Judith Kerman in Baskerville Old Face text with ITC Avante Garde Gothic titles.

Book design by Judith Kerman.
Photo of John Repp by Lori Steadman.

Contents

Then We Seemed Woven Talk

Then we seemed woven talk,
now sorrow desiccated as a moth
dead three days, wedged under a screen.

When do we stop thinking
What do you think of me?
if not when flinging words
like beads on an abacus?

The Feast of Apples.
Fetching the Mail.
Danish Fontina and Soda Crackers.
Strolling Down Murray for Milk.

The laughter last drawn thrummed deep
in our bellies, which lay taut beneath hand
or tongue or eyes dewy from day going down
to that bed again.

For the blackstrap dregs
of one dead minute
I'd what? Beg?

This sorrow will lead to more
even if we bear it, even if we get lost—
shreds of wing blown in the dust,
feathered, light-drunk, no-minded
flight itself.

No loom thumps
the rug of us. No swatches
of blue you in the sky.

I Want to Buy This House

I want to take a woodworking class.

I want to make a coffee table.

I want to make a bookcase to cover the wall where Russ and Mary Ellen
left nail-holes in the plaster.

I want to make an end table and a rocking chair.

I want to sand the chair silken, then brush on three coats of lacquer.

I want to rub lemon oil into its broad arms and set it on the porch in
whatever sun the maple lets through.

I want Victor's daughter to fall in love with New Mexico and forsake her
claim so I can make a fair offer.

I want Victor to shingle the porch roof, install a new furnace, and sign
over the house and the three fields and the wedge of Mount
Pleasant so I can screen the porch and plan the best spot for my
basil.

I want Joveen well, her scratchy voice lilting, her headscarves put away
again.

I want Victor and Joveen to stroll up their little hill in a June dusk so
violet and gold and rust they don't look at it, they kiss it.

I want the tulips Mary Ellen planted to bloom right now.

I want the peonies to stop colonizing the irises right now.

I want the bees to burr in the primrose right now.

I want a pesto dollop in my tomato soup right now.

I want to yearn for pesto in late January and two days later find a frozen
pouch behind the ice cream.

I want to stride out to the porch on January 28 bearing a bowl of linguine
and pesto, a glass of Merlot, the butt end of a homemade rye,
and every ounce of rage and bitterness I've ever drunk.

I want everyone to shut up and read Job.

I want to stop mooning about what help I haven't been, what compassion
I haven't found, what rutting I could have done but didn't.

I want never to hear another word about the New Deal or World War II
or the Han Dynasty or the Iroquois or the War of the Roses or
Ramses or Vietnam or the Progressive Era or Buddha or the
Hittites or any of the Popes or Kuwait or Freud or Angola or
Adam Smith or any other political, economic, religious,
philosophical or social entity or idea in or before the history of
this pathetic species.

I want to give Reagan his mind back, such as it was.

I want him to tell jokes and juggle and become a Lincoln scholar.
I want Lorca un-shot and singing.
I want him padding up Avenue A right this minute.
I want him to beguile every last reactionary, including the starving troll
rooting near my liver.
I want him to sing about pears and green and apricots and dust.
I want him to compliment my lentil soup and be quiet while we eat.
I want Whitman to thank me for placing a stone I found at Sleeping Bear
Dunes on the sill of his tomb.
I want him to wrestle God for eternal tickets along the Fenway Park third
base line so we can trade strophes throughout the forever 1975
season.
May Walt and Frederico be the next souls to rise from the dead.
May my neighbor split wood enough for winter.
May his daughters keep yelling my name when I ski by.
May wild turkeys feed in the snowfields.
May three days of snow squalls teach me where I live.

Another I-Love-My-Rented-House-and-the-Three-Fields Poem

After I mail the divorce papers,
the present tense lasts awhile.

I sleep twelve hours a night
the first two nights. I wake

before dawn for three weeks.
I tuck sunflower seedlings

into ice cube trays packed
with humus. I have pain

in my brow and a tree guide open
to willows face down on my chest.

——————————

Roving pack of hungers,
trolls sunk terror-struck
in their own filth.

—————————

A goldfinch dips
and rises, shadow
flickering over snow.

——————————

Four people in the rent-controlled, pre-war,
12-foot-ceilinged, galley-kitchened, sesame-

or-poppy-or-onion-bagel-for-breakfast-unless-
you-want-shredded-wheat-and-a-banana-unless-

it's-Passover apartment four floors above
100th Street read the *Times*. They bemoan the trash

around Grant's Tomb. They discuss a walk
to greet the cats at the 72nd Street Marina.

They poke at the ten-mile-high mountain
of cultural possibility. No one completes

a sentence. Everyone understands. If you could taste
the brisket and the cold sesame noodles,

you'd know what I mean.
——————————

I have a pot
of coffee hot
to my right.

Good carafe.
Good sweater.
Good fuel

feeding the furnace.
——————————

I make a bow
and light incense.

I am Whitman's age
when he soothed his boys.

Despite the photographs,
I can't imagine the wounds.
——————————

An in-law peers at my jacket,
says when he knew leather,

he could tell how long
since the animal died

and what piece of the hide
yielded what piece of the garment.

Feel the flex in this pocket.
Good leather.

——————————

To burn hard coal,
be a window.

——————————

Wind blowing waves
in clover mowed
months ago.

——————————

The facts drive
me to my knees
in corn-stubble.

Late autumn heat.
A full clothesline.
Snow two days ago.

——————————

My neighbor's green-eyed,
leg-swinging daughter asks

my middle name. I tell her.
What a funny name!

My neighbor kills a gnat,
says *Look, honey. That's a gnat.*

What's my father's name?
I say his name.

What's my mother's name?
I say her name.

We all have such funny names!

Maxine Dancing

Where is the swelter of 1969?
Where is Russian Vic with his onion and liverwurst, his fistful of stale rye?
Where is he with his shining vodka and scarlet belly and stink and square
    head shaved each morning on break?
I need the children he never spoke of and the flowers we trucked to the
    dump, how we stood knee-deep in sweetness, shoveling.
I need him in a grave troweling mortar on vault-seams, soaking the
    concrete with redolence.
I need his twelve words of English, the way he'd hose himself down near
    the Kelk mausoleum, the way he'd hang his head and whisper "Iss
    hot."
I need to pilot that Ford pickup with manual choke, hedge shears on the
    seat, Vic snoring.
I need to mow and dig and clip all day, dreaming of *The Baseball
    Encyclopedia* and air-conditioning.
I need Maxine dropping me off and picking me up, wrapping my egg-salad
    sandwich, my buttered slice of zucchini bread, bagging my chips,
    pouring my lemonade or grape juice or orange soda.
I need to refuse all help, climb on my bike and ride the five miles,
    hauling the two wet, earned dollars that become at noon a meat
    ball sub with hot peppers, fries, and a Coke.
I need Maxine hauling rocks to make the back yard home.
I need her flushed and goggle-eyed among the tomatoes.
I need her cheering or blank-eyed or raging as I sink free throws.
I need her dancing near the Wurlitzer, Lloyd Price belting "Personality,"
    my brittle mother high-kicking the backbeats, lost for three clumsy
    minutes in joy.
I need Maxine to rest and not to die.
I need her death and all the losses and joys of twenty years.
I need to un-fist these hands and tend the box elders at each end of her
    headstone.
I haul water so my father can pour it on the brown grass and the
    geraniums.
Lichen creeps from the crevices of our name.
He and I tend one another, then leave, so simple after such grasping.
I hear the noises I make, no one dancing among the ragweed and sweet
    clover in my field, no one hopping over the woodchuck holes and
    fox scat and anthills, no one spinning in the wind that carries grief
    away.

Yet

for Jan Cunningham/after Robert Hass's "Privilege of Being"

When you said   *The winter here was long*
I thought how bitter my own, how not even Hass's angels

salved the flayed meat of me, nor Rilke's Angel,
nor the angel a sweet, illiterate student swore

perched on my left shoulder, no—bitterness yowled,
a catbird blown into a scatter of rusted-out propane tanks,

clinging to a strand of barbed wire, hunkered on a radiator,
mewling at ice-fog dawn, mewling at frozen deer,

turkeys pathetic in the drifts, the fox huddled in the culvert,
screeching gray bird feasting on its own hunger,

no matter foot on foot of snow, day on day of squalls,
snapped power lines, sub-zero health warnings,

the car's low-pitched threats through April, cold May,
snow on the third of June, longing cold as the gelid tar

sunk in my poor car's crankcase, gust on gust of terror—
yet one afternoon a wood-thrush hovered open-beaked

as I riffled the book to find her. Once as the moon set,
two turkeys haggled over the cobs Bunk's reaping left.

Inside a particular minute, "I" turned his back
long enough for "me" to "know" bliss while writing

a check for the gas.

July has melted everything.
In the garden, slugs have killed the sage

a friend yanked from the bed where we stroked garlic,
pinched basil, cooed over the mint, dead sage I drove home

thriving in a grocery bag, herb Frank gave for the bed
I dug with the best shovel Agway sells—

tempered blade, ash handle, the exquisite heft
the burly clerk promised.

Five hundred miles from here, you tend snap peas,
hill potatoes and cucumbers, kneel filthy among roses,

wielding tools made to outlive us,
the only kind worth having.

Him on the Zafu

Raindog Zendo

Sap from the taproot roared
through his wooden head.

He yelled sobs.
He yowled buckets

of snot and spit.
More sap pumped.

He raged gallons
of What-About-Me.

More sap.
He spat gobs

of I'll-Show-You.
Yet more.

Each lung a bellows,
heart a furnace,

tongue acetylene.
Still more.

He stopped.
Sat foursquare

for a few seconds.

Pig

My neighbor's pigs
nap in the muck.

In a miniscule shed,
a pyramid of pig,

eyes squeezed shut,
a seeming grin on each face.

Even the piglets inside the sow
are meat. My neighbor smokes

bacon each autumn, and I eat it,
pig gist my gist.

These are the facts.
There are worse ways to wake

than in a pile of pig.

The Mouse and the Broom

The mouse cups a shred of bacon.
Nibbles. Nibbles. Nibbles.

Then the cat.
The cat everywhere.

Sit up and squeak,
eyes blood, right ear drooping.

Then the big straw doom.

Fugue

I failed to save a loved one
no longer loved. I could have done

simple things I worked to forget,
betrayal the meat of kindness,

each caress crime. Bah. Conscience:
a self swept free of cruelty,

rectilinear as the wall.
Where ruin? Where the face to blind me?

White Doe

Sleet driving down,
the white doe browses
in my rented field.

I take a step
& she bolts up the hill.

The buttery funk
of my morning beard,

the coppery tang
of my morning fear.

Out there, nothing
but wind shivering
the five leaves left
on the maple.

In here, dread
of the phone,
a friend's joke,
the power

shutting off,
the next
step. Forget
reasons. Too many

explanations.

A Zen master named Joko
calls fear paradise.

Same with all the others.
Goddamned Zen.

I prefer grief,
which drives you
to your knees when
& where it wants.

None of this
rodent nibbling.

"I prefer"!
Thick snow blows.
The wind's gaping mouth.
Childhood blanket
for heat, two candles
for light, fog
from my nostrils.

Snow to my hips,
I wade to the barn.
Near the willows, the white doe
swivels her head to whiff.

No wind, razor-cold dusk,
I stand breathing.
She bends to feed,
muzzle rooting in the drift.

Instruction

Compassion is feeling someone else's feelings and being merciful toward them.
                    A student

Stand in the frozen tire-track
past midnight. Moon, stars, no wind,
town's glow in the west. All else
the epic poem between the ears.

Up the hill, the hickory,
the spruce, the poplar & birch
crack & rattle, sway, scrape, wind
bitter & dry all day. Squeak
on new snow, corn stalk shreds, rock
maple leaves rustling. No tears.

Dig a path to the car, sun
casting jewels on the drifts.

Crows. Fox by the barn. Snow squall
howls in full sun. Propane man
pumps all four tanks full, stumbles
back to the truck. Any heat
is good heat—boiled egg, black tea,
breath-fog in the dining room.

Just past dusk, an owl hoots
on the mailbox, snow brushing
his tail feathers, wind gone, mice
& voles in for a long night.

Ithaka, this frozen place
twenty years' journey from war—

Plunder the long ship for wood.
Keep the bow strung.

Ponder the spring sowing.
Watch the harvest pass away.

Be at home for seconds, years,
awake.

Simple Pleasure

Death is the mother of beauty.
                              Wallace Stevens, "Sunday Morning"

A discarded tractor tire laid on its side,
three wheelbarrows of sand tipped in,
plastic farm animals, a corral, a squad
of Union infantry, three trucks, one front-loader

with a working scoop: the small civilization
the sons outgrew. The family moved to Ohio.
The new tenant crossed his arms. Drove to Agway
for peat moss and deodorized cow manure.

Slit the bags and shook it out. Hoed it in.
Sandy and loamy all at once. Good sun.
The tire gave shelter from the wind
everyone said got bad in August.

He drove to Agway for basil seedlings.
Dug a spoked wheel of holes, pressed the plants in
up to the first leaves. Soaked the bed down.
The season came on. He hung laundry,

pressed his face into sheets before unclipping them,
dug up the peonies, gave up trying to defeat
the woodchucks, but only after dumping
many buckets of water laced with Lysol

down the burrows. The basil grew, leaves plush
as Italian suede. The tenant pinched and watered
and wedged a leaf now and then between
lower lip and gum, chewing-tobacco

for the enlightened. Three times in dense heat
he trimmed the tangy wheel and plucked
the cut stems leaf by leaf and crushed them
with cheese and nuts and oil, all the brilliant

green genius tossed with steaming angel hair.
A frosted mug of mineral water with lime.
A glass or two of wine. Fireflies in wet dusk.
Bullfrogs and owls and peepers in full dark.

The first week of September, another trim due,
a hard frost came. Gray-green shriveled wet leaves
hanging down woody stalks in late-morning thaw.
Up to then, the tenant had eaten it all. He had meant

to freeze some. He wanted at least an echo
of basil in January. No go. He yanked out
the stalks, hoed and raked the basil tire smooth.
Mourned the royal herb killed in a white hour.

Long after he leaves, he'll recall that garden,
the playthings, the toy roads buried, meals, labor,
rubbing a leaf between thumb and finger,
the quick grief after frost, every detail

of what gets called a simple pleasure.

John Repp is the author of two books of poetry, *Thirst Like This* (1990, University of Missouri Press) and *The Fertile Crescent* (2004, Cherry Grove Collections), as well as several limited-edition chapbooks of poetry and fiction from March Street Press, Pudding House Publications, and Palanquin Press. Bedford/St. Martin's published his textbook, *How We Live Now*, in 1992. Among other awards, he has received the 2003 Lyre Prize from Cherry Grove Collections, the 2003 Editors' Prize from *Rhino,* and an NEA Creative Writing fellowship in poetry. He teaches English at Edinboro University of Pennsylvania.

Other books from Mayapple Press

Dennis Hinrichsen, *Message to Be Spoken into the Left Ear of God,* 2004
        Paper, 52 pp, $8.50 plus s&h
        ISBN 0-932412-26-2
Johnny Durán, *Nieblas de Luna/Moon Fogs,* 2004
        Paper, 52 pp, $8.50 plus s&h
        ISBN 0-932412-23-8
Adrienne Lewis, *Coming Clean,* 2003
        Paper, 30 pp, $8 plus s&h
        ISBN 0-932412-21-1
Pamela Miller, *Recipe for Disaster,* 2003
        Paper, 66 pp, $12 plus s&h
        ISBN 0-932412-19-X
Gerry LaFemina, *Zarathustra in Love,* 2001
        Paper, 44 pp, $8.50 plus s&h
        ISBN 0-932412-18-1
Judith Kerman and Don Riggs, eds.,
Uncommonplaces: Poems of the Fantastic, 2000
        Paper, 148 pp, $15 plus s&h
        ISBN 0-932412-17-3
Poems by leading s.f. and fantasy authors, including Brian Aldiss, Joe
Haldeman, Jeanne Larsen, David Lunde, Patrick O'Leary, Rick Wilber,
& Jane Yolen
Helen Ruggieri, *Glimmer Girls,* 1999
        Paper, 40 pp, $8 plus s&h
        ISBN 0-932412-16-5
Zack Rogow, *The Selfsame Planet,* 1999
        Paper, 40 pp, $7.50 plus s&h
        ISBN 0-932412-15-7
Larry Levy, *I Would Stay Forever If I Could,* 1999
        Paper, 36 pp, $6.50 plus s&h
        ISBN 0-932412-14-9
Skip Renker, *Sifting the Visible,* 1998
        Paper, 36 pp, $6.50 plus s&h
        ISBN 0-932412-13-0
Hugh Fox, *Strata,* 1998
        Paper, 28 pp, $5.50 plus s&h
        ISBN 0-932412-12-2

John Palen, *Staying Intact,* 1997
    Paper, 28 pp, $6 plus s&h
    ISBN 0-932412-11-4
Judith McCombs, *Territories, Here & Elsewhere,* 1996
    Paper, 28 pp, $6 plus s&h
    ISBN 0-932412-10-6
Kip Zegers, *The American Floor,* 1996
    Paper, 24 pp, $6 plus s&h
    ISBN 0-932412-09-2
Al Hellus, *a vision of corrected history with breakfast,* 1995
    Paper, 24 pp, $5 plus s&h
    ISBN 0-932412-08-4
David Lunde, *Blues for Port City,* 1995
    Paper, 24 pp, $5 plus s&h
    ISBN 0-932412-07-8
Evelyn Wexler, *Occupied Territory,* 1994
    Paper, 80 pp, $10 plus s&h
    ISBN 0-932412-06-8
Evelyn Wexler, *The Geisha House,* 1992
    Paper, 24 pp, $5.50 plus s&h
    ISBN 0-932412-05-X
Judith Minty, *Letters to my Daughters,* 1981
    Paper, 24 pp, $5 plus s&h
    ISBN 0-932412-04-3
Toni Ortner-Zimmerman, *As If Anything Could Grow Back Perfect,* 1979
Paper, 16 pp, $5 plus s&h
    ISBN 0-932412-02-5

Also available through Mayapple Press:

Judith Kerman, *Plane Surfaces/Plano de Incidencia*, 2002, CCLEH
    Bilingual, translations by Johnny Durán
    Paper, 144 pp, $15 plus s&h
    ISBN 0-932412-20-3
Dulce María Loynaz, *La Carta de Amor al Rey Tut-Ank-Amen/*
The Love Letter to King Tutankhamen, 2002, CCLEH
    Bilingual, translation by Judith Kerman.
    Limited edition, of 250, signed & numbered.
    Paper, 28 pp, $10 plus s&h
    ISBN 0-932412-24-6

Judith Kerman, *Mothering & Dream of Rain,* 1996, Ridgeway Press
Paper, 88 pp, $12 plus s&h
ISBN 0-932412-22-X

Judith Kerman, *3 Marbles,* 1999, Cranberry Tree
Paper, 32 pp, $7 plus s&h
ISBN 0-9684218-1-4

Judith Kerman, *Driving for Yellow Cab,* 1985, Tout Press
Paper, 16 pp, $5 plus s&h
ISBN 0-932412-04-1

Sample poems and the latest information for all Mayapple Press publications are available online at *www.mayapplepress.com*